IT'S
SO
ME

Written by

Lorraine M. Williams

Bald Girl Inc. Publishing

Library of Congress Control Number: 2020918854
Copyright: @2020 by Bald Girl Inc. All rights reserved.
ISBN: 978-1-7358245-0-5
E book ISBN: 978-1-7358245-1-2

Cover Design: Austin Weatherspoon | AustinGraphix | Austingraphix@gmail.com
Edited by: Tiphane' L.M. Purnell | Success Dealers International, LLC | successdealersintl@gmail.com
Formatted by: Success Dealers International, LLC
Photographer: Celeste Jones I celestejonesphotography
MUA: LaRee Gould
Author: Lorraine Williams

Ordering Information:
Special discounts are available on quantity purchases by corporations, associations, and others. For details, contact the publisher. For orders by U.S. trade bookstores and wholesalers contact the publisher at info@baldgirlinc.com.

Printed in the United States of America.

Dedication

I dedicate this book to everyone that brought the lie that they were not enough. Be encouraged! You are enough, and you are beautiful just the way you are.

Shout Outs

To God be the Glory! All things are possible with you!

There are several people I must thank for helping me get this book out.

I would like to thank Carla Saratt, Yvette Gaines, Fairly Hopkins, and Camilia Jones for being my second set of eyes. Thanks for not having your girl out here looking crazy.

Thank you to my big sister, coach, and friend, Cheryl Pullins. There would be no Bald Girl without you. Love you!

Thank you to Shanae Dell for your constant support and friendship. This book might still be sitting on the shelf if it were not for you. Love you Sunshine!

Tiphané Purnell, thank you for being obedient to the call on your life. Had you not answered the call, this book might have not been here.

I am forever grateful to God for my parents. He knew this crazy child would need a little extra care, so He assigned me to you.

You guys will never know how much I love and appreciate you. I am here because of you!

Lastly, thank you to Team Williams; Calvin, Khaleah, and Kyra. I am so grateful to God for allowing me to be on the team. Your love and support allow me to be me. I love you to the moon and beyond. You guys are THE BEST!!

Table of Contents

Forward

"**P**lease don't touch my hair." A very "touchy" subject for black women: Pun intended.

Regardless of the type of texture, length, or being fully bald, when it comes to hair, black women have a deep emotional connection to it. It has even been reported that black consumers spend nine times more on ethnic hair and beauty products than our non-black counterparts.

Why such a deep emotional connection to something as "simple" as hair?

That's exactly what *It's So Me* delves into. This book provides a transparent and vulnerable glimpse into what it looks like when your hair takes on a life of its own, and when it even begins to control your life.

Often times, when we see a woman rockin' a bald look, we have two schools of thought. One thought is, "She must be having a health issue." The second thought is, "Wow! She is trying to make a statement."

But what if it's neither? What if she struggled with her hair so much that wearing a bald look was more than an act of bravery, but actually an act of unapologetic freedom?

The freedom to fully be herself and walk in her truth, without permission, apology, nor sympathy.

Cutting all your hair is not the courageous part of the decision. Deciding to no longer allow your hair to define you, is what really takes courage.

Why? Because it's a fact that, as black women, we are judged by our hair, but even more so we are categorized, as well, both inside and outside our ethnicity, and opposite gender. From pretty with the brown eyes and long hair to not so pretty with the big lips and nappy hair, and everything in-between, we will be judged.

But what happens when you decide to make your hair a non-factor? When you decide to remove it from the equation? Yet, others react as if you've broken a cardinal rule.

When someone is brave enough to take a stand for herself, she then gives others permission to take that same stand for themselves. This book is not designed to make you feel good. It comes from an authentic place with real pain and experiences, and has been written to empower you to make choices for yourself; not only about your hair, but about anything that suffocates you and attempts to stifle you, or make you a non-factor in the world.

Some decisions are scary, yet freeing, but living in the reality of freedom is empowering.

Even though you don't need permission, it's something you crave, and what Lorraine has done in the upcoming pages of 'It's So Me' is that she has given you permission to 'be so you'.

Oh, Gorgeous and Beautiful One, you were created to live an incredibly fabulous life, whether you have a full head of long flowy hair, short curly hair, or you decide to go completely bald.

I love you, sis! You were destined to do marvellous things in this world! You are not your hair.

You are a woman who was fearfully and wonderfully made, and your hair has never been nor will it ever be the deciding factor.

Cheryl Pullins
CEO & Principal Brand Strategist
Iconic Persona, LLC

Prologue

Recently, lawmakers passed the Crown Act, making hair discrimination illegal. The effect of this new law will be far reaching as many black men and women can now be allowed to wear their natural hair, the way it grows out of their scalp, without any discrimination. Ain't that about a 'B'! Hair plays such a significant part in the lives of people. It is an accessory that speaks on our personality and on who we are. For black people, hair also speaks on where we've come from and the history associated with it.

Society has continuously dictated what is acceptable for black people; from how we dress, where we live, and the state of our hair. We were taught that our natural hair was unacceptable for years. We were made to believe that it was nasty, nappy, and ugly. When our ancestors were stolen and brought to America, our natural hair was one of the things they could not steal. Something began to change as our women were raped and started producing mixed-race children. The children's hair had a curl pattern that was not as tight as ours, and they had a skin that was lighter. The lighter you were, the more favored you were. This birthed the idea that the lighter you are with longer, straighter hair, the better you were. White was perfect: Black was shameful. The lie started then, but it was passed on from generation to generation. If you wanted to fit in, you needed to conform and make yourself acceptable to those holding power and those in control. However, those people did not look like us. They tried to take our hair as a form of punishment, but we found a way to make the loss of hair an avenue for our freedom.

We were told that we were beautiful and appeared kept when our hair was pressed or chemically treated to look straight instead of the tight curls that grew from our scalps. Light-skinned was pretty: Dark-skinned was not. Long hair was beautiful: Short hair was not. So, where does the bald black girl fit into all of this? Where does the black girl who cannot grow hair fit into this equation? Is she not beautiful because she does not have long straight hair? Hell, is she not beautiful because she does not have hair? Of course not. But why does she feel the need to conform? The need to attempt to fit in to be accepted by not just the society, but from the community that should welcome her for the mere fact that she is them? How do we change the narrative? How do we go beyond our natural hair being a fashion trend to simply a way of life? Why are you proud of me or call me bold because I choose to stand in my natural state?

Introduction

Hello! Hello! Hello! And welcome to It's So Me. I am your host, Lorraine Williams, with Baldgirlinc.com, your redefining beauty consultant, and I am here to share my story. Some of you may know me as Lorraine, others as Bald Girl. Either way, we are the same. You may think you know my story, but you have no idea. I decided to write this book because I often get questioned about how I evolved into Bald Girl.

Now, for those of you who don't' know me and you saw that fly picture on the cover of this book and thought to yourself, She is killing that "hairstyle", I did not set out to make a fashion statement. I have an autoimmune disease called Alopecia Areata, which causes my hair to fall out, and there is no cure. As a black woman living with this disease, it can be difficult and challenging because we put so much emphasis on our hair. In some cases, our hair dictates how we act and live, and we restrict ourselves based on the time between our next hair appointment.

As a black female with no hair, who has decided to take control of this disease, I decided to shave my head. With this type of Alopecia Areata (there are several types of Alopecia), my hair grows in patches, and then it falls out in patches. Honestly, that is a little too much for me to handle regularly, so I just decided to shave it as it grows to cut down on the drama in my life. I shave it daily to keep it neat, and to stay cute. Although I keep it fly, this was not my ideal "hairstyle" – this journey was long and stressful. I initially did not want to deal with this disease, and I covered it up for years. Covering up is how we handle challenges that may come up in our lives that we ignore and hope they go away. But you know you can't put a band-aid on a bullet hole and hope it heals.

This book is me being open and honest with the reader about my journey to transforming myself and discovering who I was, and what I was placed on this earth to do. We all were born for a specific purpose, and all of us have an assignment to fulfill on this earth. Our assignments are explicit to our journey, and God gives grace for that assignment. Could it be that frustration sets in because we are off task and not on purpose? Your reason for living on this Earth is of a bigger purpose than you know. Someone somewhere is waiting for you to tap into that greatness. Someone needs what you have, and if you aren't in place, you could be someone else's delay. You are not helping anyone while pretending to be someone/something you are not. Do you even know who you are? Why you are here?

I believe we go through different challenges in life to be able to help someone else. No, it doesn't make sense, and during the process, it sucks. But God created us for a reason. I had two choices; continue to fight the process or accept my assignment. Purpose fuels you to do what you are called to do. It is grace that allows you to do what seems easy. When I finally accepted I had Alopecia, I understood my purpose was to help others find their inner beauty. I knew it was my responsibility to share my story and show women what is possible, and that those possibilities go beyond any life challenges.

Psalms 139:14 says, "I will praise You, for I am fearfully and wonderfully made." I have grown to love the shape of my head. My peanut head is perfectly shaped because God chose to use it as part of my calling. After losing my hair, it took years before I could look at myself in the mirror and see myself as beautiful, but I can tell you that today, that there is no day that goes by that I don't look at myself and say, "you are beautiful." It took me a long time to get here, but I am grateful to God that I am here

I Dream of Hair

Growing up, I spent countless hours sitting in the beauty shop, watching my grandmother transform women's hair. They would come in looking one way and leave looking totally different. The women that came in and out of the beauty shop had all types of hair: Long hair, short hair, grey hair, blonde hair, black hair, brown hair, matted hair, almost straight hair, and so on. They were all different, but one thing they all had was hair. I watched as my grandmother would wash and blow-dry her clients' hair. Pressing out the natural curl pattern to transform their locks to a head full of silky hair.

My grandmother was a magician. She owned a salon and was known as a "master presser." Rain and humidity were no match for my grandmother's press. She would get the pressing oil on that "kitchen" and gently blow, while the heat and the oil would darn near burn the skin off the back of your head. I still remember feeling the coolness of her breath, blowing on me, at the exact time the heat from the straightening comb was setting me on fire. Her gentle blow would quench the burn. The smell of that hot comb meshed with the pressing oil filled the air. It was a combination of the magic oil, heat, and my grandmother's technique that made women feel and look beautiful. Although she was a magician, she could not give me what I really wanted – long hair.

Me and my hair have had this love-hate relationship since I was born. Most babies in my family were born with a head full of curly, soft, and dark hair. That was not my testimony. I came out the womb with dry, ashy 4C hair. I had the tightest, dullest, dark-brown curls. If you were ignorant, you might have said my hair was nappy. Thank God my mother was a stylist too, and she made it work. Any baby pictures you see of me are of a cute little girl with bows attached to the top of her head, putting on a big smile.

If someone had asked me if I had good hair or bad hair, I would have probably said I had cute hair. People labeled you with good hair if your hair was long and straight. I guess I had bad hair because mine was anything but long and straight – my hair was short and super tight. Most of my friends had "good hair," and I remember wanting my hair to be long too. My hair wasn't like my friends', but my mom used what I had to make me look nice. My parents always affirmed me. They always told me I was pretty, and that my hair looked nice. Although my hair didn't look like my friends', I believed that it looked nice as my parents said it did. I don't know if we realized the lesson that was being taught growing up, but it helped me to be ok with being different.

I was never the girl with the long flowing hair. My ponytails left a lot to be desired, so I didn't wear them often. My mother kept my hair in what we affectionately called "city blocks." When done right, it looked like a cluster of neat row houses, lined on city blocks. The only good part about that hairstyle is that my hair was nice and neat, and it helped my hair grow. My "city blocks" always ended with pretty bows or cute barrettes.

The week before my first-grade school picture, I scrapped up my face. The tiny street we lived on was lined with poles about 4 feet tall and spaced six feet apart. All the kids on our street would spend hours jumping over them, up and down our street. My mom had just warned me to stop jumping over them, but I had to do it one more time. As the saying goes, "a hard head makes a soft behind." In this case, my hard head had me falling and landing straight on the right side of my face. I ran into the house, bleeding and crying. My mom immediately cleaned me up and made me stay in the house for the remainder of the week. The next day, the freshly scraped skin was a mix of pink and brown patches where my face met the pavement. The week before, I lost a tooth right in the front of my mouth. As crazy as I know I looked, my mom said, "You're so cute. Your picture will be adorable." I believed her and took that picture with a big smile. The color on my face was back, but I was missing my front teeth and wearing a green sweater. My hair was pressed and up in a ponytail with a white ribbon. And yes, I was adorable.

What also worked in my favor was that I was cute. Not to sound like I'm feeling myself, but I was. I had dimples, and my mom kept me in the cutest outfits. Although my hair was never long or flowed in the wind like most of my friends, it eventually grew to about mid-shoulder when I was older. It was short and tightly coiled for the most part. I also did not have a relaxer. Now, what you need to understand is that I grew up in the inner city; girls were getting their hair relaxed before leaving grade school. Because my grandmother worked magic with the hot comb, I would get my hair pressed, and the younger stylist in her salon would cut and style it. So, no one knew the difference.

People can be petty, and petty people have petty kids. As a kid, I learned early to just do me. Some would love me, and others would not. Either way, it was not my problem. I remember when I was going into the 5th grade, girls were getting their hair braided and adding small plastic beads to the braids' ends, securing them at the bottom with rubber bands or small pieces of aluminum foil. Adding additional hair to the braids was not as common as it is today, so the girls with the longer hair had long braids, and their beads made rattling noise as they swung their heads back and forth.

The Saturday before school started, my aunt decided she wanted me to get my hair braided. She was friends with an African woman who braided hair, and she added hair to create longer styles. Now, this was huge back then because there were no braiding salons, unlike today where braiding salons are a dime a dozen. I was excited to let her braid my hair because I was finally going to have long hair. I remember picking out the tan and brown wooden beads she would attach to the ends of my braids from a bowl she had on her table.

She braided my hair into this Cleopatra bob, and instead of using foil to secure the beads, she burned the ends. I had never seen this done, so when she pulled out a lighter and put the flame near my face, I pulled back and looked at her confused. She told me to relax. Securing them with fire made the beads look seamless. She flicked the lighter, at the same time grabbed one of the braids, and she began to touch the braid with the flame. The smell was different from when my grandmother pressed my hair. The smell was more like plastic meshed with hair grease. It smelt horrible to me, but it sure looked nice. When she finished, she gave me a mirror to look at myself. The braids were gorgeous, and once again, although others had braids, no one had braids like me. I was ready to start the 5th grade.

Going to 5th grade meant Middle School. Middle School has grades 5-8. I was a little nervous but excited to go to a new school. Lunch was divided into grades. The 5th and 6th graders had lunch together, and the 7th and 8th graders ate together. About a week into school, at lunch, a 6th grader came up to me and my new friends and said, "You think you cute, don't you?" I said, "Yes, I do," and laughed. She responded with, "Let's see how cute you are at 3 o'clock when I beat you up," and walked away laughing. I froze. My new friends looked as scared as me. No one said anything. We all just stood there, looking crazy. All I could say was, "She wants to fight me?" I was about 5' feet tall and maybe a 100lbs. She had to be about 5'5" and 135lbs, and she was top heavy. This was not going to end good for me.

The rest of the day, my stomach was in knots. Every five minutes, I'd look at the clock in fear. I had never been in a fight, and I wanted no parts of fighting this 6th grader. She was older and bigger, and I was scared. My mother would kill me for fighting in school, and my dad would kill me if I ran from a fight. I had to decide, and time was ticking. Three o'clock was coming fast. The dismissal bell rang on time, as expected, and my decision was made. I grabbed my backpack and burst out the side door, running the mile and a half home in a panic top speed. I never looked back. I don't think I've ever run so fast in my life. As I approached the steps to my house, completely out of breath, the first thing I saw was my dad washing his car. Winded, I stopped running, and with a look of terror on my face, our eyes locked. He knew without me saying a word that something was wrong.

Now, to put this in context, my father is a third-degree black belt. Sensei Jones, as his students lovingly call him, was a no nonsense, over-protective, loving husband, and father. With your natural eye, he's not intimidating at all. Barely, 5'8 and 170lb gentle spoken man; you might sleep on his ability. Because my father taught karate, by default, I learned to fight. I had spent hours with my dad, learning from him and sparring. Under no circumstance was I allowed to start a fight; it was strictly for defense. More importantly, I was not allowed to walk away from one.

When I arrived home that day, out of breath and fear on my face, he immediately asked what was wrong. Lying to my parents was a waste of time, they had some Ninja discerning gift for sniffing out a lie, so there was no point in lying. Getting caught was already guaranteed. I took a deep breath and told my dad what happened - all of it. He calmly turned the water off from washing his car, grabbed the bucket, and said to me, as calmly as he could, "Ok, well, you are still going to fight today." I looked at him and said, "I don't know where she lives." Walking towards the house, he said, "That's ok. You are still going to fight today." I followed him in the house, and he told me to meet him in the basement. My mom tried to save me and said, "You don't have to go," but my dad, still with his calm voice, said, "Yes, she does." Talking about dead man walking, it was really about to get crazy.

Our basement had sparring mates and all kinds of pads for fighting laying around. My dad was already in the basement, putting on his pads as I slowly walked down the steps. He was putting on the pads the students used. I stepped on the mat and he looked at me, got in his fighting stance, and said, "Let's go." I paused (obviously too long), and he popped me in the arm with his glove. Tired from running and frustrated from being afraid all day, I freaked out and started swinging my arms in a windmill motion and kicking my feet wildly, like I had lost my mind. I was completely out of control and was not landing any hits. Meanwhile, my dad was moving all around, tagging me at will.

After what felt like an hour, feeling defeated and exhausted, I almost gave up when I heard my dad's calm voice, "Where's your training?" Suddenly, I remembered what to do. All those hours I spent in the basement with my dad came back to me. I do not think I understood the training until that moment. To me,

I was just spending time with my dad, but he was actually teaching me and equipping me.

I calmed down and fought like my dad taught me to. Once he saw that I remembered his teaching and technique, the "fight" was over. He took off his gloves and said, "Remember your training. You have no reason to be afraid. I always have your back," and he walked up the steps. I stood there for a brief second to take in the day, and that moment changed my life. I was never afraid of anyone ever since that day in my life. At that moment, I realized he had fully equipped me to handle any opposition that would come my way. This lesson would carry me through many life challenges. This training was the start of the knowledge, posture, and confidence to help me realize my hair was not my defining factor.

The next day, I went to school as usual with a newfound confidence. At lunch, the 6th grader I ran from the day before approached me with a cocky smile. Before she could utter a word, I punched her in the face. BOOM! As hard as I could. She stumbled, and I began to unleash a beating on her like she slapped my mother. I don't remember much detail about the fight; it was like I blacked out. Once I regained my consciousness, I remember someone pulling me off her, and a crowd of kids had gathered, yelling, laughing, and clapping. I don't remember hearing anything or noticing there was a crowd until then. As the person grabbed me off her, my hands were in a tight fist. As I released my fist, one of my hands was full of beads. The sound of the beads hitting the ground shocked me. They belonged to the girl I was fighting. She wore her hair in braids too, but with the plastic beads and aluminum foil to secure them. I walked away unscathed, and with all my beads still in place.

I was ushered to the office and made to sit in a chair near the door. My heart felt like it was beating out of my chest. I kept thinking to myself; my mom is going to kill me. My mom is a small petite woman – 4'11" probably 120lbs, but she is not to be played with. She could grip you up and lay you out before you even realized she was coming. She didn't play when it came to school, and my dad would not be able to protect me from my mother's wrath. I was afraid and mentally exhausted. I really could not handle two days of this kind of stress. The door opened, and a man walked in. He was one of the NTAs that worked at the school. He was the one who pulled me off the girl. He looked at me and smiled, and said, "Don't worry. You are not going to get in trouble. I handled it, but you will have to stay here for the rest of the day." I looked at him in relief, but also slightly confused. He said, "I know your father. I know you didn't have a choice," and he let out a small laugh.

When the dismissal bell rang, the NTA dismissed me. I grabbed my bag and took my time, and I slowly walked home. When I arrived, my dad was sitting on the steps, waiting for me. He said, "what happened"? I said, "I fought her." He smiled. Although he didn't say it, I know he knew what happened. As we walked up the steps together, my mother was sitting on the porch, witnessing our conversation. I smiled at her and said, "Hi, Mom." She looked at me. She was not happy, but she said hi and turned her head. She was pissed with both of us, but that day, at that moment, I didn't care. I was proud of myself, and so was my dad. I had learned so much in those two days that I only wanted to enjoy the moment. This lesson taught me to be fearless. It helped me to be confident, knowing that I was well prepared to handle whatever might come my way.

Mom and Dad

Me and Dad

Me, brother, and mom

Transformed

I did not get my first relaxer until my freshman year of college at Cheyney University (the first HBCU-PERIOD!). I was sitting on the floor in my dorm in Tubman Hall. I don't remember who, but one of my friends was slapping relaxer on my hair and smoothing it out, while a few of my other friends watched. It was about six of us in the room. Suddenly, I felt heat. As every second passed, the heat felt hotter and hotter until I felt like my entire head was on fire. I remember the girl putting the relaxer in my hair kept saying, "Hold on! It's almost done," as she continued to work that liquid crack through my hair. Finally, I couldn't take it any longer. I jumped from the floor and bolted to the door. "Leave it on!" My friends yelled! "It's not done," as I ran down the hall towards the hall's bathroom sink. As the cool water washed over my head, I prayed that I still had hair. The heat was overwhelming as I doused the flames with the hose from the sink. Eventually, the water quenched the fire that was burning on top of my head. Silky strands of straight hairs began to lay draining on my forehead. I no longer had to go home and get that fresh press from my grand mom. This relaxer made managing my hair so much easier. This was the beginning of my hair transformation.

Up until that point, my hair, other than it not being long, was healthy. No breaking, no shedding, no problems. For the most part, my hair just went along for the ride during my college years. It was healthy, so it could take a little beating. I now call this my "Grace Period." In my senior year of college, I started leaving campus to get my hair done. My stylist, at the time, did hair in the basement of her mother's house; they had set the basement up like a small salon. There was her workstation, a washing bowl, two hooded dryers, and a couple other chairs lining the wall for people to sit. She was finishing up cosmetology school, and after classes, she would come home and do hair. When she arrived home from class, a few of us would be outside her house, waiting for her to come home and do our hair. The first time she styled my hair, she cut my hair into this cute pixie cut. A little length on the top, short on the sides, and tapered in the back; it was so dope. By this time, I had embraced the fact that my hair was short. In fact, this new cut took it (my attitude) to a different level.

My last spring break, me and a few of my friends drove to Florida (actually, another confession, my friend Kareemah drove back and forth because she was the only one with a driver's license at the time). We laid on the beach, partied, ate, and got tattooed. My short sassy hair cut was the perfect addition to our wild trip. We continued the party for the remainder of the semester, making memories that would carry us for years to come; all that partying came with a price.

The last few months of my senior year was a nightmare. I went through a bad breakup, and just as the semester was ending, I found out that I was not graduating. It was time for me to pay for all that partying. I had taken an internship between my Sophomore and Junior year for 12 credits. It was not required, but my aunt insisted I get an internship. She felt it would be the only way I'd get a job after graduation, majoring in Criminal Justice (she was right). She orchestrated an internship with the City of Philadelphia, working with the Juvenile Probation Department in West Philadelphia. My advisor agreed I could use it as department electives. I never got it in writing, and I was too busy having fun to follow up. The credits showed on my transcript with 4 As, and that was good enough for me. By not getting it in writing, when the department did its audits for May's graduates, I was short 12 credits and was not graduating.

I was devasted! While my friends were planning graduation parties and preparing to walk across the stage to get their degrees, I was packing up my things and moving back home; without my degree and four years of debt. I remember spending time in my room, feeling heartbroken and defeated. My parents didn't freak out. They drove up, helped me pack the car, and took me home. They welcomed me with open arms and showed me love when I needed it the most. By the end of the month, I was over myself, and I decided I needed a change. My stylist told me she had a style she wanted to try on me, and I gave her go ahead. She dyed my hair red and shaved it off. I had this cute tapered cut that I'd have to get trimmed weekly. All I had left was a bang (and that was a weave track). It was short and sleek, and I was the only one rocking this dope cut. I loved it!!! It was so freeing, so refreshing, and so me! Short hair was definitely me!!!

I became addicted to changing my hair. I think I was searching for the rush I felt when I cut my hair the first time. The thrill of a new hairstyle felt like conquering new territory. Each time I changed my hairstyle, I felt like I was discovering a part of myself I never knew. I was unintentionally a trend setter; I would try anything, and the stylist that did my hair loved me. Around this time, I had a few people doing my hair. Anytime they wanted to try a new style, they would call. I would wear my hair short, long, black, brown, blonde, or red. It didn't matter. It was just hair, and if I didn't like the style, I could change it. If I couldn't grow it, I could sew it. I remember when I got engaged, and my grandmother said to me, "Girl, your husband ain't going to ever be able to recognize you. You're always changing your hair." To this day, I still enjoy and get excited about a new do; only today the excitement is a little different.

A month before my wedding, I noticed a dime sized bald spot towards the bottom left side of my head. My hairdresser and I chalked it up to wedding nerves and didn't worry about it. We gave that area of my hair a break until the wedding by hiding it under some weave. For the wedding, I wore a shoulder-length, glued in, full weave. My bridesmaids wore their hair braided up into regal crowns. I remember being slightly jealous that my hair was too short to wear the style, but I was happy that my girls looked amazing.

Shortly after the wedding, I noticed that my hair was a little thinner in one area than the rest. Other than my hairdresser, no one else noticed. We did a couple of treatments, but the problem did not go away. I rarely, if ever, wore just my hair. I remember an incident where I was having a weave removed and the shampoo girl ripped the track from my scalp. The same spot that I had notice the difference. I let out a loud "ouch!" She apologized while massaging the area, but the damage was done. My hair was never the same in the spot again.

As time went on, I started noticing other areas of my hair changing. It was not as thick as it used to be, different areas were a lot stronger and thicker than others. I decided to take a break from the chemicals and just "go natural." I thought I needed to get back to my "roots." Instead of wearing my own hair (which was now too fragile), I wore braids - All kinds of braids; Micros, Kinky twist, two strand twist, knots, you name it, I wore it.

I took a shot at locking my hair. This had to be my most favorite hairstyle. The Loctician added some hair to the locks (because you know I had a thing for length). My hair appeared to be growing, and I was excited. So, a few months into the locking process, some of my locks started to snap close to my scalp. They were nice size locks; not too thin, and definitely not too thick; they were perfect. Well, at least that is what I thought. But this was not good. Apparently, my hair could not take it. My so called "Grace Period" was up.

With no other option, I went back to wearing braids. My hair, however, decided it already had enough of all these hair games. The sad part was that I didn't care. Ok, let me clean that up. It was not that I didn't care that my hair was falling out (because I did), but I was more concerned about my appearance. By now, I was married with two daughters. What was I supposed to do? I had to look a certain way. My hair was always a part of who I was! My only concern at this point was camouflaging my head until my hair grew back. I figured I was safe because I wasn't using any chemicals. Because I took this passive approach, the situation gradually got worse, and I settled with wearing a mask, pretending to be ok.

First, my sides became extremely thin; the slightest tension broke them. Then there was a section at the crown of my head that began to fall out. Slowly but surely the area of weakness and breakage grew. At first, it was the size of a quarter, then it spread over time like the plague over a large section of the crown of my head. At this point, I could no longer go without a weave of some kind; it was literally impossible. Did I mention I was in my early 30's? This was devastating.

I finally went to see a dermatologist. I set my appointment for the day after I was to take out my braids. I went to the doctor with my hair wrapped in this fierce headwrap. I remember thinking that the doctor would give me some type of "magic" cream and prescribe some pill, and I'd be on my way. You can image the horror I felt when the doctor told me that there was not much he could do, and that I should stop wearing braids and just let my scalp get some air. "So, wait a minute, you want me to go outside like this?" I said. "It's not bad," he said. Did he have any idea of who he was talking to? I left his office crushed. The next morning, me and my fierce headwrap were sitting in the chair in the braiding salon doing what I did best – covering up what had now become my shame.

This went on for years; I went back to wearing weave. At some point, I was introduced to weave caps and wigs (affectionately called girlfriends). I figured I could go back to wearing my "city blocks" under my cap or wig until my hair grew back, and I'd be ok. For a while, this seemed to be working. There were some signs of growth, not a lot, but there were some. I remember one day that I decided to try a relaxer. Don't ask me why! I had worn my hair short in the past, so I felt comfortable with my decision. WRONG! It looked crazy - See through hair with random patches. The misfortune was that my scalp was done with me, and it refused to be abused any longer and checked out. Literally! Within 2 weeks, I was back under the influence and embracing my camouflage. Can I have my weave please?

Me, my mom and my sisters Tanya and Lanaye

Mommy and M

We wear the mask, that grins and lies

Can you imagine finding out that you have this disease that there is no cure for? It's not going to kill you, but it is going to take your hair away, and there's nothing you can do to stop it? Oh, and by the way, limit your stress because that can aggravate it. WTH!! Now imagine, you are the type of person to move in silence and who is too prideful to ask for help, so you walk through this season alone – without your tribe.

Now, let me say that I have some amazing people in my tribe, who would have rallied around me with the support that I needed. If I am honest (yes, another confession), my personality is not set up to ask for help. It's something I'm working on now because I realized I needed others. This was the time that I really needed my tribe, to come in full force. I could have asked them to come over with all their shenanigans to help me to just take a pause. Just for a moment, to forget all the pain I was feeling and just be with my girls. Christel would have shown up filled with positivity. Shanae, who would have been knocking on my door with a bottle of my favorite wine and a healthy snack. Kareemah would have talked me into taking a run to clear my head. Stephanie would have come up with a good idea to make some quick money. Nikki would have just talked to me and made me think of other things. Anika would have had me out in my garden, getting me back to nature. Angie would have made me laugh until my stomach hurt Fairley would have been my champion and convinced me that I could handle this and everything else that came my way. My spiritual mom, Yvette, would have prayed me through this storm like she has some many other times in my life. Cheryl would have let me vomit all over her and then helped me back to good emotional health. My mom would have sat with me and listened intensely to me talk with my head on her shoulder, while she's silently praying. My sister, Tanya, would have held my hand and cried with me. I needed them at that moment and I, for whatever reason, didn't ask for help, and I chose to struggle alone.

While I was mourning the loss of my hair, my family was going through some major issues. My marriage was a MESS! Our relationship was hanging on by a thread (that is another book). In a last-ditch effort to save our marriage, we decided to relocate to another state. We decided that moving would be good for us to start over. Our new house was beautiful. It was the cutest house, in the middle of a cul-de-sac, that backed up to a wooded area. It was on a quarter acre of land with a pool, a double deck, and a swing set for the girls. We were in one of the best school districts in the state, and the development was filled with children our daughters could play with. It seemed like the perfect place to reconnect and raise our children – until the bottom fell out.

Two months after moving, I lost my job. When we moved, my husband and I kept our jobs, which meant we had long commutes. My commute was two hours, one way, and my shift started at 6am. My company had an office closer to where we lived, and my supervisor thought I would be picked up by that office. Unfortunately, as soon as I was laid off, our company entered a hiring freeze. We were now in this new house, with one income.

Just when we were adjusting to one income, my husband lost his job. Losing my job was not a huge hit. It was inconvenient, but we were able to make it. But when my husband lost his job, it was catastrophic. My husband had great credit and a six-figure salary. Initially, we were completely shocked. We did not panic because we knew we would be ok financially for a while, because my husband was great with managing our finances and saving. We believed that we both would be back to work soon, and we'd be fine.

Well, things did not go as we thought they would, and it took us longer to get back to work, and when we finally did get back to work, we were not making nearly as much as we needed. Eventually, the well dried up and the savings were no longer there. I remember coming home one day after picking up the kids from school, to find a foreclosure note on the door. My heart sunk! Remember, I'm supposed to be limiting my stress! Yeah, ok!! I ripped the note off the door and quickly rushed the girls in the house. I remember trying my best not to lose it in front of the girls. I set them up at the kitchen table with a snack, and I told them they could watch a little TV before doing their homework. I ran upstairs to my room and bust out crying. I called Calvin and told him what I found. He told me not to cry and that everything would be ok. But I was a mess the rest of the day.

We filed bankruptcy and tried our hardest to keep our house. First of all, we lost my car. The repo man came to our house at 3am, banging on the door and shining bright lights on our house. Remember, we lived on this quiet cul-de-sac, and this man was out there making a scene. I was so embarrassed. My husband got up and out of the bed, and he went to the garage opener and let them in. They turned off the lights and took my car. I cried myself to sleep.

Fortunately, my husband worked for a car dealership and he had a loner from the dealer. We lived in a rural area, and a car was a must. Having one car was difficult, but we were grateful to have transportation. At this point, I had no idea what was coming, and I honestly was not ready. We struggled to make the bankruptcy payments. We were working, but the payments were difficult to make. Two years after filing for bankruptcy, we lost our home. Devastated does not adequately describe what I felt. I could not believe what was happening to my family. We had lost everything we worked so hard for. Our cars, our houses (we had two), and that A-1 credit my husband once had was shot. If it were not for our faith, we would have lost our minds; not to mention each other. Even with my faith, this changed me.

Now, when this happened, we were ministers, which in some way posed a whole set of other problems. We had learned to trust God as our source, and He had blessed us beyond our wildest dreams. We were not just saying it or teaching it, but we were a living proof that the Word worked. We were sold out and then we entered what I call "our Job" season. Here, we are teaching about faith and being obedient to God, and eating the good of land, and our land had appeared to be dried up!

At this point, we just decided to believe that God would see us through. We may not have had everything we wanted, but we were desperately in need of anything. We were at peace with God – at least that is what I said in public. In private, I was secretly feeling like God had left me hanging and that I was paying for something I did on the back end. My mouth was making all the right confessions in public, but I was not 100% sure that God was with us. In addition to me losing my hair, my family had now lost everything.

A month before we left our old house, we had no idea where we were going. My husband came home one night from work and just sat outside in the car. He said he sat there and cried. He did not have a clue what we were going to do, and I was in no position mentally to help him figure it out. It's not easy to move with a fresh foreclosure on your report. It was at that moment a neighbor knocked on the car window and asked if he was ok. This neighbor used to talk to my husband often about some challenges he was having with his wife. He said he saw my husband sitting in the car and came to check on him.

My husband is not big on sharing his feelings. He is private and does not share personal things with anyone, but this was different. He felt led to share what we were going through. The craziest part was, the neighbor came over to talk to my husband about a house that his wife had purchased, and they could no longer afford to pay both mortgages. He was looking for advice. Look at God! This was an answered prayer for both men. He offered to rent us the house and of course, we accepted.

It was two full years before I was even able to drive pass the development of our old house. It was very painful. After we moved, I did not want people to visit. Entertaining and having people over was something I used to love to do in our old house, but that feeling was gone. This house was a really nice townhome in a town not far from our old house, but it was not my house. I felt like a failure, but I could not tell anyone. My husband had resolved that there was a lesson to be learned, and that if God blessed us before, He would bless us again. Because what he was believing and saying was better than what I was thinking, I just keep my mouth shut and suffered in silence. All during this time my condition was worsening.

One night, after moving, I had a horrible dream. In the dream, I left for work in the morning and I went through my normal daily routine. Work, grocery store, church, pick up the kids, and back home. Normal. However, everywhere I went, people were staring at me with the craziest looks on their faces. Some people even frowned and looked disgusted. It made me feel uncomfortable. It was so awful. I had no idea why people were looking at me that way. In the dream, we were living in the first house we owned. At this house, we had a large glass front door;

one where you could see your reflection almost like looking in a mirror. I looked at myself in the glass and I was also horrified. I began to scream hysterically, and I woke up. Then I began to cry. My husband grabbed me and asked repeatedly what was wrong. Once I was able to compose myself, I told him the dream. In my dream, I had gone all day, outside, without my "girlfriend" (my wig). The world had been exposed to my shame. My mask had been snatched away! I immediately sunk into a deep depression.

Season of Job

Depression creeps: it does not happen overnight. It slowly seeps in and begins to set up roots. Like weeds in a garden, if left unattended, they begin to spread and blend in, and eventually take the over. Weeds choke out the healthy things that are supposed to be growing, making it difficult for them to grow and multiply until they die. Weeds are hard to kill. You can pull them up when you see them, but they pop out every time it rains. Until you kill the root, they will always return and multiply. Sometimes, the weeds could have been allowed to grow for so long that they have time to go deep, which makes them difficult to get to. It takes time and energy to get to the root, but when you do, your grass/garden's true beauty can shine!

When I finally accepted that fact that I was losing my hair, I felt helpless. As a young woman, I felt like I was losing an important part of my being. As a black woman, I felt devastated. We have spent countless hours in beauty salons and kitchens and spent billions upon billions of dollars to ensure that our do's were right. It does not matter if you are natural, chemically treating, or you weave your hair, you have contributed to this mega industry. Losing my hair felt like I had almost lost my black-girl membership.

I kept thinking to myself, "what am I going to do?" I had to accept the fact that my hair may never come back and I needed to choose to either shave it off and be completely bald (I was almost there), or wear some type of hair prosthetic for the rest of my life. **THE REST OF MY LIFE??** At this point, I was 35 years old, and the thought of a life sentenced to weaves and, or wigs was just heart breaking. I was not ready to make that type of commitment. Then I thought about my husband. He would never be able to run his fingers through my hair (Although that is a no-no in our community). I could not let him see me, ever, without my hair. Even though he knew what was going on, I needed to spare him, and myself, the embarrassment.

As strong and as fearless as I was, this part of my personality did not align with how I felt about my husband. I knew my husband loved me, and he was physically attracted to me, but would he feel the same way if he saw my shame? What would he say? How would he feel? Would he try to pretend to be okay, or would he hate it and feel some type of way? Would he lose interest? I had created all kinds of crazy scenarios in my head. We had worked hard to save our marriage and I was fearful of what this would do to us. I had worked myself up so much that I began to believe that if he saw the real me, he would walk away, and I could not afford to lose him too.

Wearing a full head weave is expensive. From the buying of the hair to the installing and maintaining, the cost can a bit much. I had been weaving my hair for a while, and with our financial situation at the time, my hair choice was not in the budget. Somewhere after losing our house, I started watching You-tube tutorials on wig reviews. I was looking for cheap wigs that looked good. One day, I bumped into a girl doing a short pixie weave, with weave called 27 pieces. She had a short pixie weave. Had I not seen the before and after picture as the advertisement, I would have never known she was wearing a weave. I cannot tell you how many times I watched that video; I studied it like I was going to be tested. I studied her technique. I watched it so much that I knew what she was going to say. Finally, after watching her video for about a month, I was ready to try it.

I went to the hair store and purchased the hair, the glue, and a hair razor. I took my purchases home and locked myself in the bathroom. I washed my hair and conditioned my it while I watch my You-tube girl one more time before I started. I laid the hair and glue out on the counter, and I propped my phone up so I could see. I started the video again and began. I used my husband's clippers to give the back of my hair a smooth tapper. The back of my head was the only part of my hair that seemed to not be affected by Alopecia. I measured out the placement of each track just like she did – one track at a time. I measured, cut, glued, and laid the track, layering it as I went around my head.

Once the weave was in, I took the razor and began styling the hair. I started around the ears because it was easier. I then moved up the right side to taper it some more, and then to left, and finally the back. I used my fingers to guide me. I stayed locked in that bathroom for two hours straight. Once I was done, I stared at myself in the mirror, and I loved it. After that day, I spent two hours every two weeks, held up in my bathroom with the door locked. The door was locked because I did not want anyone to see the condition of my hair; it was horrible. Patches of hair in some spots, bald spots in the other. Every time I took the weave out and saw my actual hair, I felt ugly. I wanted no one to see me like this, including my husband. Thank God we had two other bathrooms in the house, so there was no reason he needed to come in. He never challenged me on it. I think he understood I needed space to work through this. I felt bad not allowing my husband to see me like this, but there was no way I could look at him again if he saw my shame. So, I hid it. As far as he was concerned, my hair was not an issue. He sympathized that I was upset about my hair, but he never treated me differently or stressed over it, and he really did not like when I did. He would let me have my moments, but he would not let me wallow in them. He knew that I needed to deal with all the emotional baggage that came with this loss, and he couldn't do it for me.

Then I thought of my daughters. I did not want them to have to go through this. What kind of example was I setting for them? I knew there were some generational issues here. My mother suffered from hair loses as well, but she was comfortable with her "girlfriends." I just was not ready to deal with any of this. I had learned to master masking my feelings (So I thought). But they would just manifest themselves in other ways. I was angry, I was sad, and I comforted myself with food. At some point during this hair journey, I began to pick up weight. At first, I did not notice it. Then, over the course of a year or two, it was becoming obvious that I was growing – literally! I remember when I was a little girl, I was very thin. When puberty kicked in, it settled right on my behind. When all my friends' breast began to grow, my behind began to swell. My breast did not begin to grow until much later. I envied them because they all had boobs (and hair), and all I had was this big ole booty.

Because I had to carry this big trunk, my hips and thighs had to grow to carry it. I had a tiny waist, small breast, hips, and thighs, and I was 12. It was cute when I was a teenager and in college.

When you are young and always moving, it is easier to maintain. I had learned to appreciate my gift and used it to my advantage. Males loved that thing. Between the dimples and that big behind, it wasn't too hard.

As I got older and started having children, it was a little harder to keep it all together. With all the drama that was going on, (loss of job, hair, and house) it was the last thing on my mind. I only really thought about my weight in the summer when it was hot. I remember slowly going up in size. First a size 12, 14, then 16, eventually a tight size 18 (I was not buying a size 20). Although I was going into the store and purchasing the clothes, I honestly did not "see" how big I was. I never weighed myself, so I really did not have a clue how much I weighed. I think there were just too many other things going on for me to really notice. For the most part, I thought I looked the same.

I began to come to terms with my hair issue. I started talking about it to people as the Lord led. Every time I told someone, I felt like some of the weight had been lifted. I was not healed of the pain, but I wasn't afraid any more to at the very least talk about it. I also started allowing my daughters to see the damage. I felt like they needed to see what I was going through; I needed to share my story with them. I didn't walk around parading it, but when I removed the weave, I no longer locked the two of them out of my room until I was done. I let them come in and see. I think it helped all of us. It opened the dialogue about hair and how each of us felt about it. I looked forward to our conversations. They both felt like I should just cut what was left of my hair off, and that the weave was not helping. I knew they were right, but I was not quite ready to go that way.

Every year on my children's birthday, we let them choose what they'd like to do. Both of their birthdays are in the summer. My oldest daughter usually asked to go shopping, and my youngest always wanted to go to an amusement park or the beach. Whatever they decided, we all went as a family and spent the day celebrating the birthday girl. One of these celebrations changed my life forever. It was my youngest birthday, and she decided that she wanted to go to the Six Flags. She and I are roller coaster junkies. The bigger and faster, the better. It was a perfect day for riding. We arrived at the park early and got in line. Our favorite coaster (King Da Ka) was closed for the day, but there were still plenty of coasters to be had.

My husband isn't really into to riding the coasters, but he'll do it for the girls. They start him out slow with the mild coasters and work him up. They usually question his Marine-ness, and he feels like he needs to show them how they do it. Mid-way he usually quits. When we got to the third coaster, we got in line and waited for our turn. My youngest and I love to sit in the front, but we decided not to wait (the line is usually longer in the front) and just went to the first available. This particular coaster sat four to a row in individual seats. We sat down and got ready to be thrilled. We were so excited, and our adrenaline was pumped! The arm rail came down and you are supposed to pull it all the way down to your waist, and then it clicks. The attendant comes by each person and pushes the rail further down into your stomach, and it clicks again.

When the attendant came to me, he pushed the rail and then asks me to sit all the way back in my seat. I replied, "I am." He said, "Ok, let me try again." He pushed again and whispered to me to sit all the way back. Again, I told him I was, and that I couldn't go back anymore. He attempted to push the rail one more time but there wasn't any more room for me to move back. He couldn't get it to click. So, he whispered to me that I would have to exit the ride...WHAT? Do I really have to get off the ride - in front of everyone? He didn't want to make a scene, and not even my family knew what was happening, and they were sitting with me. I got up and got off. My youngest daughter yelled, "where are you going, what's wrong?" And I told her to go ahead and I'd meet them at the exit. The attendant saved me and told them he was having an issue with the seat, and that I told him that I would get off as not to hold up the rest of the guests. I gave him a nod and walked off the platform.

Inside, I was crying like a baby. I had never been more embarrassed in all my life. Never had I felt so humiliated, and I had no one to blame but myself. As the ride pulled off, I remember feeling like such a failure. I was thinking to myself that I had no idea that I was "THAT BIG." Was I really that heavy that I would need to be put off a ride? I wanted to disappear. I was completely and utterly devastated. With all these emotions overtaking me, I didn't even realize the ride was over and now, my husband and daughters were now standing in front of me, wanting an explanation as to why I got off the ride.

I don't know how I was able to get the words out without falling apart and bursting out in tears. I told them that the attendant could not lock the bar rail, so I had to get off. Of course, one of them wanted to know why he couldn't lock it. So, I said because I was TOO big. ***Silence***. It seemed like I shut the park down with that statement. I'm sure it was only a couple of seconds, but everything seemed to stop moving, and there was complete silence. After their initial shock wore off, they all attempted to say things they thought would make me feel better. But none of them helped.

My youngest said, "Oh well, mom, let's just get on another ride." I said to her without even hesitating, "I'm done – I'm not riding anymore today." She looked disappointed and walked off to the next ride. Her sister went with her. My husband wasn't really okay with what I said or how I looked. So, he said, "I know you're not going to act like this all day. I understand you are upset but you don't want to ruin her birthday. You know she wants you to enjoy the day with her and ride."

My flesh took a stand! If I had a gun, I would have shot him. Really Calvin? Didn't he know I was hurt? Didn't he know I was completely and thoroughly embarrassed? I was not riding another darn ride, and if he knew like I knew, he would leave me alone. I turned to him and said, "You don't know nothing! I'm not riding anything! You do it!" He looked at me and said, "Ok, it really isn't a big deal. It is her birthday and you shouldn't act like this the rest of the day." I did not say another word. The girls got off the ride and I walked away. My youngest came over to me and said, "Are you going to ride anything with me?" I said, "I'm sorry, but no. I'm too big and I don't want to be put off another ride." She answered, "It's ok."

The rest of the day was crazy. When you are at an amusement park, you are usually there all day, and other than walking and riding, what else are you doing? Eating! This was one of the last things I wanted to do. Of course, that was not going to last because I was hungry, and so was everyone else. I don't remember eating. I remember thinking I did not need to eat anything – ever again. What has happened to me?

I had sunk deeper into my depression. It was bad! Depression had become a part of me, and this issue was just additional fuel. The bad part of depression is that it never comes alone; it brings its ugly twin, Oppression. They stalk you like a Ninja day and night. Their only assignment is to steal your joy and paralyze you! My joy account was darn near depleted. I knew this was not healthy, but I had no idea what to do, and I could not tell anyone how I felt. Now, I am not only losing my hair, renting a house from someone, working at this low paying job, but I was now fat. I had walked around sulking and feeling disgusted with myself being nasty to my family and having an attitude with everyone at work

I had not realized it, but food became my drug of choice. It made me feel good even if only for a few minutes. I could not talk to anyone about how bad I felt. I could not talk to my husband because he had enough on his plate. I could not talk to my friends because I was embarrassed. I could not talk to my parents or siblings because I was ashamed. So, I put on a mask and pretended to be ok, while I comforted myself with food.

Because I did not want to deal with or think about all the things that was happening to me, I numbed myself with food. Addiction makes it hard to function. The problem with being addicted to eating is that, unlike alcohol or drug addiction, you have to eat. Food is meant to be fuel, and I was abusing it; instead of dealing with the things that were hurting me, I ate.

For two weeks, I walked around beat down. I did not want to do anything or go anywhere. I did not want to see or talk to anyone. I just wanted to stay in my bed, sleep, and cry. Depression had fully taken over. Then I remember getting ready to cry myself to sleep one more night, and I decided I was tired of crying. I just laid there staring at the dark ceiling. Just then, I realized that I had decided to do nothing. In my doing nothing, nothing would ever change, and everything would remain the same. And because I was not doing anything to change, depression stayed around.

Trouble with the Twins

Growing up, the two things I wanted were the two things I did not have: long hair and boobs! Some of you think this book is about hair, but beauty is multi-faceted. We all seem to want what we can't have. As we were wrapping up my yearly female exam with my doctor, she calmly proclaimed, "Welcome to the 40's. Now you can add needing a mammogram every year to your schedule." She recommended I have it done where she gets hers done, and I scheduled my appointment. Two weeks later, "the twins" were being squeezed between a human vice grip as the rest of my body attempted to hold the weird position the tech required me to hold in order for her to get that "just right picture." The "machine" brutally compressed my right twin like I would a bug underneath my shoe; or the way I would squeeze a lemon to release its essence. No mercy! I was literally forced into the torture chamber by the tech five times. Five times the machine literally squeezed my twins to a pulp. To her credit, the tech was as pleasant as she could be, and if I had to have it done, I'm glad it was with someone whose spirit is full of life.

As she wrapped up and released for the final time, what felt like a death grip, she said that because it was my first mammogram, the doctor may request additional pictures. She assured me that it was routine with "virgins" and not to be concerned if I received a call for additional pictures or a follow up visit. Not a problem. I got dressed and apologized to the twins for the abuse.

A week later, I got a call. The nurse said that the doctor noticed 2 small lumps in my right breast and was requesting that I schedule an appointment in another office to have some further tests done. She said not to worry, and that because this was my first mammo, the doctor had nothing to compare this one to, and she gave me a number to call to schedule the mammo and ultrasound. This was a call I couldn't say I really wasn't expecting. When the tech mentioned that I might get a call, I kind of figured that was a polite way of saying she saw something and to "expect a call." Although I was somewhat in shock, I knew enough to not speak any negative words (although they were rolling up in my throat). I called Calvin and told him what happened, and he said, "Praise God." "WHAT?? Praise God???" I asked in shock. Then he said, "Yes, I'm thanking

Him in advance for keeping you." He continued, "You don't have anything to worry about." I knew he would help me focus.

The day of my appointment, I arrived early at this Imaging Center. A few minutes later, a little bubbly woman came out. She was friendly enough and took me down a long hallway. When we got to the end of the hallway, she put me in this small room and asked me to undress from the top up, put on a gown with the opening in the front, and she told me to have a seat when I was done. After I was seated, she came in and took me into another room. The "torture chamber" was center stage. She began to explain that they had seen two lumps and wanted to examine them further. The torture began. She began to torment my right twin. She was literally abusing it. I felt like I was being assaulted and she should have been arrested. The grip was so intense at one point that my reflexes almost kicked in, and I felt like I was going to back hand slap her. That wasn't even possible with the tight hold that machine had on my twin. I was too afraid to pull away. It may have ripped her off!

The suffering went on for about 30 minutes, and she initially took 5 pictures. Pulling and stuffing, squeezing, and tugging...ugh. Simply horrible! And for someone who was lacking in this area, this whole process was a struggle. After she told me she was done, she left to show the doctor the films. She came back 10 minutes later and advised that she needed to take another picture. But get this, in this photo shoot; the left twin got to be violated too. GREAT! I was thinking 'you've got to be kidding me'. The best part...we played this part of the little game 4 times before the doctor moved me over to get the ultrasound.

She took me to another room and there were two techs waiting. The room was cold, so the twins were standing up at attention. One of the techs began to apply this warm gel to the right twin. She started to probe my twin with this rolling instrument. She was probing and probing. She kept on probing, and when I thought she could not possibly probe anymore, she probed some more. I felt violated. She placed a hand towel over my twin when she was done, and said she'd be right back. I asked if I could get dressed, and she told me not yet, that she needed to show the pictures to the doctor, and she may want additional photos.

When she returned, she told me that the doctor wanted additional photos and the probing started again. Unbelievable!! Once again, she placed the towel over the twin when she was finished, and she told me she would be back. As I laid on the table, I was thinking there had got to be a better way. Women have been having this done for years and we still have to get tortured when we visit these doctors. Something more humane should have been developed by now.

Think about it. Our yearly GYN exam is no walk in the park. They lay you on this table, make you spread eagle; with your behind darn near hanging off the table. Then they tell you to relax as they place a metal instrument inside you. Then when you just get used to the cold temperature of the metal device, they place a small brush, of all things, inside. Oh, but that couldn't possibly be enough. Once they remove the metal instrument, they decide to totally violate you with their fingers. How rude??? Then when you somewhat get use to this abuse, you turn 40 and they introduce you to "the machine," and a new form of torture begins. I am convinced that a man invented all of these humiliating and painful devices; so called preventive test. Only a man could possible think these means of testing is ok. I guess my question is after all these years and with so many brilliant female doctors and scientist, why hasn't one of them devised a more pleasant and less invasive testing methods? I'm just asking.

As I was getting caught up in my thoughts, the techs walked in. I was now informed that the doctor would like her to probe my left twin. You've got to be kidding me? She started the same process on the left side. She then left the room again, and 10 minutes later, the infamous Radiologist walked in. She was about my age; possibly a year or two younger. She came and stood directly over me (all in my space), and she informed me that the original film showed 2 lumps. She said although she saw them, they could be a cyst or really nothing at all. She'd like me to come back in 6 months to have them examined again. REALLY?!?!?!? You want me to come back here and knowingly subject myself to this foolishness??? Really?!?!?!

I left the office frustrated, sore, and bruised from my encounter with the "machine." I called my husband and gave him the horror story. Again, he began to thank God that I was whole. We talked for a few minutes, and he asked me if I was ok. I told him that I just needed a minute. I called one of my girlfriends and asked if she wanted to do a little retail therapy. She always makes me laugh, so it was good to just hang out. We had a bite to eat before leaving for home.

In the morning, I received a call from my GYN. She advised me that she wanted me to see a breast surgeon right away – no later than next week. A BREAST SURGEON??!?! You just said that you believed the lumps were cyst?!?!?! What does that have to do with the swollen intruders under my arms??? She gave me a couple of numbers and told me one of the offices should be able to see me soon. She also told me that they were requesting a CAT scan of my chest. So, I made the appointment for the next day with the breast surgeon. The Breast Center, as it is called, is at the Cancer Center at Christiania Hospital. I called Calvin and told him what was going on, and as usual, he was calm and reminded me to stay focused.

On the day of my appointment, I arrived at Breast Center, found the Surgeon's office, and signed in. Once I was done, I was whisked off to an examination room and asked to undress from the waist up, put on the "uniform," and advised that the doctor would be in shortly. The last two times a nurse gave me those same instructions, the twins got the "smack down." But since the "machine" was nowhere in plain view, I reluctantly undressed and had a seat.

A few minutes later, the Surgeon came in. He was a character. Well-seasoned – could be my grandfather. He reviewed my chart and said, "You just turned 40?" I said, "Yes." He then looked over the entire test and said, "My God, they really did a number on you." You think?!?!? He went on a tangent about how sometimes a "radiologist" panics and orders all these tests, and he was sure I had nothing to worry about. He was very gentle in his approach, yet he was very thorough. He began to explain things as he rubbed and poked. He then had me lie on my back and examined the lower part of my arms. He said he felt things, but he was not overly concerned. He helped me up, and he told me to get dressed and meet him in his office so we could look at the films together.

When I arrived in his office, the first thing I noticed was the numerous awards and degrees on his wall. I knew he was seasoned in age, but the accolades plastered just about everywhere speak volumes as to his creditability. He told me to have a seat and pulled up to the huge computer monitor that was on his desk. The moment was short-lived as it was time for the "Feature Presentation" in HD, starring the twins. The right twin was the main character – the left twin played an almost silent supportive role. There were so many pictures on the film that even the doctor said, "they really tortured you." Thank you for acknowledging. What I also appreciated was that he explained every film, and he spoke in regular folk's terms. Not trying to talk over my head – pausing and asking if what he said was making sense and waiting for a response. He showed me the areas of concern from the Radiologist. They were small nodules, or what I like to call suspects, that I wouldn't have picked up in my monthly self-exam. We examined all the suspects in both twins. There was a small gang of them under my arms. A few had twins of their own that were on top of each other.

There was one suspect that he was a little concerned about. It was a little over 3 centimeters, and it had the shape of a small lima bean. It was black and appeared solid. The surgeon's speech began to speed up just a tad when he discussed it, and he quickly went to another slide with a suspect he wasn't as concerned about. I asked him what made him more concerned about one than the other, and he explained that the others weren't as defined. This one appeared completely solid all the way around without a break.

He sort of gave me two options. He said I could tell him 'I'll see you in four to six months' and wait it out to see what happens, or we could take the aggressive route. He then immediately began to explain this procedure he wanted to do. He said he would numb the twin and extract fluid from the suspect. If it was solid, then he would take a piece of it and have it analyzed. Although he said these were options, I really didn't feel like I had an option. He thoroughly explained the process (right twin ultrasound with aspiration – left twin ultrasound with possible aspiration), while looking me square in the face and only briefly pausing to fill out paperwork. When he finished talking, he walked me to the office, and I scheduled, for the following week, what the receptionist called "Biopsy times 2" to the scheduler on the other end of the phone. After the schedule was done, she gave me my papers and instructions for next week, and she asked if I had any questions. I wanted to say, 'I'm sure I do but darn you folks don't give much time to process or digest anything around here'. Geesh!

I arrived on time for my procedure. The surgical suite was right in the front of the building, so I didn't have to go far. I entered and there were women of all ages, races, and sizes waiting. A few minutes later, a nurse came and whisked me to the back. I asked if she could bring my husband back when he arrived, and she apologized but said that only women are permitted in the back as we walk past a room full of women in the worst shade of pink robes.

The tech greeted me and explained what they were going to do, and that she was going to start with the ultrasound of the left twin. As I got up on the table, I noticed a large tray full of several large needles and a couple of other instruments that lay perfectly on blue colored paper. I was cold, so of course the twins were once again at attention as if they were expecting a visitor. The technician was thorough but gentle. She got the pictures she needed of the left twin quickly. Then she cleaned up the twin and began the same process on the right. Just as she was done cleaning up, the doctor came in to begin the process.

He looked at my chart and joked, "My God, we have a lot of work to do today." I didn't really find that funny, but he made further comments about there being a lot going on, and he said there was nothing to worry about. He explained everything he was going to do, and the process began on the right twin. As I braced myself, he applied pressure to the right twin, and I felt a prick, then a slight stinging sensation. He located the first intruder; another one was hanging out with it, so he told me he got a two for one. Apparently, they just pop at the slightest prick. He seemed pleased. He did this four additional times.

Each time he got one, it was like a small celebration of achievement.

Once he was done, he bandaged the twin up and showed me one of the tubes he had placed one of the intruders in. It was the smallest little thing. It looked like a piece of thread or string. The fluid looked like contaminated water. He cleaned up the twin and wrapped her with gauze and tape, then he shouted, "Great job, now let's get the big one." THE BIG ONE?!?!?!? Uhm...no one told me. Throughout this point, I thought the drama was with the right twin!?!?!?!?!?

He made a joke that he needed to set the mood, and he dimmed the lights in the room, just allowing enough room for him to see exactly what he was doing. The left twin was front and center in the spotlight, ready for its solo performance. He told me that for this one, he was going to use a very thin needle. After he numbed the twin and started, he said that there was a huge vein near this intruder and that he would have to go around the vein to get it. When he reached the intruder, it moved. Every time he tried to get it, it moved. Finally, he decided to numb it more and try a different approach.

During the left twin's procedure, he was not telling jokes. He was pretty quiet, except when he needed the technician to move or hold the camera. When he couldn't get a hold of the intruder, he told me that he was going to use something else, and he grabbed a different instrument and went back in. I felt more pressure than I felt before, and he was really concentrating. This time, I felt a little discomfort. There was a burning and sharp pinching sensation in the area he was working on. Finally, I heard a loud POP! It startled me and I sort of jumped. He calmly said, "ok," and he pulled the needle out only to go back in again – two more times. Each time, the popping noise almost made me jump off the table. He was finally done, and I looked as he was passing the ultrasound instrument to the nurse; it was covered in blood. She removed the protective cover and smiled at me.

The doctor commended me for doing a great job. He said usually, there are not that many intruders to take care of, but I handled it well. He showed me the needle he used and said that it collected some pieces of the intruder to be analyzed. The needle was long, and the syringe was half the size. I really didn't know what to make of everything. The tech lowered the table, helped me up, handed me my clothes, and told me to take my time getting dressed.

One of the first things she told me was to leave all the bulky bandages on until the next day and not to shower. I thought, "Did she just tell me not to wash?" I said, "Excuse me?" She repeated herself and said I could not wash until the next day. Anyone who knows me knows this was not going to happen.

Telling me not to bath is like ordering Jesus not to heal on the Sabbath. She must have noticed the look on my face, and she told me that the gauze cannot get wet, so I was left to use my best judgment. Perhaps a sponge bath...right. Before leaving, the nurse told me I should hear from them in two days. The two days came and went, and I was fine. I went about my normal duties and didn't worry at all.

The following Monday, I called the doctor to see if my results came in. The nurse told me the cysts were benign and that everything looked good. She told me I still needed to come in for my follow up appointment just to make sure everything healed correctly, but I was fine. She said the doctor would probably call me later in the afternoon to go over the details.

When he finally called, he said there was no cancer found in the right twin, and everything was good there. He said the results from the biopsy for the left twin had not come back yet. I refocused, took a deep breath, and told myself that it didn't matter what they'd tell me, I would be healed. I said a prayer and thanked God for my covenant of healing, then I called Calvin.

For some reason, I felt good. I was not worried. I was not scared. I was not the least bit concerned. I felt at peace. It was like taking in a deep breath of fresh air after being stuffed up in an old cramped room. Or more like the feeling of raindrops on your skin on a hot summer day; it is so refreshing. I knew, without a shadow of a doubt, that God had me. It is hard to explain the feeling, especially after everything I had been through in the previous few years. There was such a peace that came over me. I knew at that moment that no matter what, everything was alright. I was completely resting in God. I had nothing to show or prove that all was well, but I felt good. I knew I was healed. I thanked God and went to sleep. That was the best sleep I had in a long time.

The next day, the doctor called. He said he finally got the rest of my results, and all was well. I thanked him and smiled. When I hung up, I just said thank You. I thanked God for His faithfulness. This was the best gift I had I ever received. Right up there with the gift of life. I was so grateful!

Peel and Heal

The incident with the twins changed me. I had been so concerned with my hair, my weight, and everything, I lost myself; I had not dealt with anything that was happening to me. I was just suppressing my feelings and eating. I was a mess and I was getting on my own nerves. I remember crying out to God, asking Him what was wrong with me, How I got here, and as I was praying, God brought to my memory something my husband would always say. "God would only do what we cannot do." We are waiting on God to do something, but He has already equipped us with everything we needed. He is waiting on us to tap in.

I brought Calvin a treadmill one Father's Day. It was being used as a clothes holder in the basement, so I decided that I would use it. I started walking three days a week for 20 minutes. My knees were really hurting, but I refused to quit. After about a month, the pain was becoming a problem, so I decided to go see my doctor.

The first thing that happens when they bring you to the back at the doctor's office is they walk you to the scale. I am no fan of the scale, and I always make it my business to inform the person who asks me to step on it. I removed my shoes and reluctantly stepped on the scale. I knew I'd gained weight since the last time I'd stepped on a scale, but I wasn't ready for what I saw. The nurse pushed the knob over to 200lbs and then began pushing the other knob to the right – past 210, 215, and 220, and then rested at 225; two hundred and twenty-five pounds!!! I was speechless.

I turned and looked at the nurse, and I asked if she had her foot on the scale. She smiled and said, "No, that's all you." I was speechless. I could not believe what I was seeing. I had been walking for a month and watching what I had eaten for a month, so I knew I probably weighed more when the episode occurred at Six Flags. I was so upset with myself.

The day I gave birth to my youngest child, I was 199lbs. I was now 26 more pounds than I was when I was nine months pregnant! I was almost sick. I felt depression creeping up, but I said a quick prayer, took a few deep breaths, and followed the nurse down the hall. The nurse took me into the exam room and the doctor came in. I explained to him my knees were really bothering me, and he said, "It's because you are carrying too much. You really need to lose some weight." ***Blank Stare***

I remember thinking I wanted to haul off and slap him, but I put my flesh in check and said to him, "That's what I am trying to do!!"

I explained to him that I had been walking and it was becoming a pain, and at this point, the pain was becoming a bit much. He said that the only thing I could do was slow down my pace, use an ice pack, and take Tylenol, but if I wanted to lose weight, I'd have to move. I left the office somewhat disappointed. It took everything in me not to give in to my flesh's cry for French fries. Instead, I decided that I really needed to make some changes. I wasn't taking care of myself. I was caring for everyone but myself. My husband and kids were my priority, but I would be no good to them if I couldn't take care of myself; I was finally tired of being tired.

I was 38 and it was a month before my 39th birthday. I decided by the time I was 40, I would choose to love myself – for real! This was one month prior to my 39th birthday. I set some goals to reach by the time I was 40. I would lose 40lbs (one pound for each year), become a published author, run an organized race, and finish my degree.

Two months later, I was still walking 3 times a week, but without the pain, and now, I was going to the gym twice a week. I changed my eating habits and was headed in the right direction. I had stopped stressing over my hair and was concentrating on getting healthy. By November, I had co-authored a book and I felt great; I checked off one of the goals. I had given myself a whole year to lose 40lbs. I really could not see beyond that. Four months in, I hit my goal. For the first time, in a long time, I felt strong; mentally, physically, and spiritually.

All was good, but a big chunk of my time was spent managing my hair. The weave was not lasting as long as it had before, because I was working out. I was sweating like a cow, so the weave needed to be changed more frequently. Those two hours I used to spend in the bathroom were now a luxury I no longer had. Now, every time I took the weave out, I considered cutting my hair off. It was so much work maintaining the weave with my new schedule, but every time I looked at my actual hair, I could not imagine cutting it. I decided to visit a dermatologist to get some advice. It had been over 10 years since I last saw one, and maybe some things have changed.

The day of my appointment, I was nervous but anxious to see what the doctor would say. I took out my weave and wore a cute head wrap. When the doctor walked in, he introduced himself and asked me a slew of questions. I was holding my hands tight. My palms were sweating, waiting for the moment I would have to show him my head. Finally, the moment arrived, and he asked if he could see. Reluctantly, I removed the wrap. He gently began examining my scalp – slowly touching my bald spots and feeling what hair was left on my head. This exam seemed to have gone on forever. He did not say one word while he examined me. When he was done, he removed his gloves, grabbed a little rolling chair, and pulled up in front of me, then he looked me straight in my face.

He said, "Yes, you do have alopecia." I looked at him and almost got up to walk out. I could feel my anger welling up, and right before I blasted him, he said, "But let's try to treat it." There is no cure for Alopecia, so I was intrigued by how he thought we could treat it. He said he wanted to do cortisone shots directly into my bald spots. The cortisone had shown to stimulate growth in some patients. It would not fix it overnight, and there were no guarantees, but he was willing to try if I were. I would need to visit him monthly to receive these shots, so I agreed to try.

He got up and left the room, and he returned with a tray containing several items on it. He changed his gloves and prepped for my injections. He then prepped my scalp by cleaning the areas to be injected. I had bald spots all over my head, so I got really nervous. He could sense my nerves and asked me to relax, take a few deep breaths, and let him know when I was ready to begin. As he spoke to me, the needle was in his hand. I closed my eyes and took a few deep breaths, and I said a silent prayer. I then told him to begin.

The first injection was near my right temple. It felt like a sharp pinch and then a flash of heat. Before I could take another breath, he had injected me an additional two times. He moved quickly around my head and injected each spot. I lost count around 25 shots. It took everything in me to not pass out. This went on for what felt like forever. When he was done, he said I did good, and he'd see me next month.

I do not know how I made it to the car, but I remember sitting there in a daze. Confused with head tingling as if it had been on fire, I called my friend, Angie, and told her what happened, and that I was in shock. She talked to me until I was able to get myself together, and I drove home. For the remainder of the day, I was not myself. I kept thinking to myself 'what are you doing'.

I did this for three months straight with no change. The day before my fourth appointment, I decided I wanted to see what my head looked like without hair. I was curious. I had worn short hair but never bald. I would have had to take it all the way off to even it out. I grabbed my husband's clippers and went to work. I cleaned off the remaining hair in about 5 minutes. I looked in the mirror and to my surprise, it wasn't bad, then I grabbed a wig and went about my day.

The day of my appointment, I wrapped my head in a cute headwrap and went to see my doctor. I had decided that morning that I was going to tell him I would not be taking the injections any longer, and that I was going to leave it alone. We had no success and sitting through another round of painful injections just did not make sense. When he walked into the office, I was sitting there without my headwrap. It was the first time anyone had seen my bald head. He smiled and said, "Wow, I think you look nice. Are we really going to go through the injections?" I told him no, that I was done with the injections. He smiled and examined my scalp to see if there were any signs of change. He then looked at me and said, "I agree. No more injections for you."

Team Williams

After every doctor's appointment, I talked to Calvin. But this time, I didn't know what to say. I had decided that it was time to deal with this hair issue. I could not let Alopecia and the fear of what people thought of me control me. The only way I could take the control back was to cut off my hair; I would be the one in control of whether I would be bald. Now, the only thing left to do was talk to my husband.

I needed to do it before fear would talk me out of it. All those scenarios I created were playing like re-runs on television, and I needed to speak my heart before they won. Instead of having several conversations, I decided to call a family meeting. I told Calvin and the girls I needed to talk to them. They could hear the seriousness in my voice. I am sure they thought it was something much more profound than what I was about to say. They sat together on the sofa, with Calvin in the middle, bracing themselves for what I was about to say.

I told them I was tired of playing the hair game and I thought I was ready to cut my hair off, but I also I needed to know how they felt. As much as I was over this hair thing, I did not want to create unnecessary stress for them. My personality does not allow me to be on the fence; I'm either in or I'm out. If I was committing to this, I was going all in. The girls were in high school, and I needed them to understand that I would be showing up with a bald head. I did not want them to feel like they needed to explain what was happening or have to deal with people making fun of their mother. Then I turned to Calvin. He was on verge of starting a ministry and church; people can be funny. The church folks were going to have to be comfortable with his wife being bald. It had taken me way too long to get to this point, and I was not going to allow these people to force me back into hiding. I shared with him my concerns about going out and people staring, or his friends not understanding. I just dumped all my trash and stood there.

They all looked at each other and Khaleah said, "This is what you wanted to talk to us about? Me and Kyra told you to cut if off years ago." Kyra said, "Just cut it off (almost like she was irritated)." They began to give me back what I have told them since they were little girls. They reminded me how I told them that they were beautiful just the way they are, and no one defines that for them, and they did not need to prove anything to anyone. They said, "Take your own advice mom." They threw shade, but I was proud. Calvin sat there, taking it all in. When the girls were correcting me, he said, "You have to do what is best for you. The only thing that matters is you are happy. If this will make you happy, then do it. If you are not happy, we won't be happy." I love that man!

Can you see how, in not taking control of your thoughts, you can be on the express train to crazy town? The Bible says to "cast down all imaginations, and every high thing that exalts itself against the knowledge of God, and bring into captivity every thought to the obedience of Christ." You cannot just allow yourself to meditate on any and everything. My thoughts led me to believe my husband's love for me was superficial, and that my family would not understand what I was going through. I created this false expectation that appeared real, and it costed me years of unnecessary pain. I felt blessed that they supported me and pushed me to embrace myself fully. I do not believe I would be where I am today without their encouragement. They made it possible for me to finish the work that I had started, and to settle in on my decision.

Now, if I was going to rock this baldie, I needed to enlist some help from one of my Stylist friends. I called my girl, Angie. She was the only one who had seen the bald spots, and I trusted her. I called her and told her I wanted to cut my hair, and I wanted her to do it. She paused and said, "Nah, I can't do it." I darn near begged her, but she wanted no parts of it. She just kept saying she could not do it. Then she said, "How about you let my barber do it." Angie wore the back of her hair tapered and her barber kept her taper dope. I took a deep breath and said, "Let's do it." She scheduled the appointment and the date was set.

The day of my appointment, Angie picked me up to take me to my appointment. I wore this cute headwrap in a tight bun. When we arrived at the barber shop, there were a few guys sitting in the shop being serviced. Angie's barber greeted us, and I sat in the chair. Before I took off my hair wrap, I told him, "just make it nice and neat," and then I removed the wrap.

With Alopecia Areata, the hair falls out and grows in patches. My patches looked like random patterns of different sized polka a-dots all over my head. My hair does grow, but it grows in patches. Dealing with the patches is hard, and it was just too much emotionally, so keeping it cut would keep me from having to be bothered with them. Although I had cut it myself, I wanted a barber to cut it the right way, and I'd maintain it.

When I removed the wrap from my head, the barber took a few seconds to look at it before saying anything. He said, "Uh, what do you want me to do with this." I wanted to be offended, but I understood his confusion. I said, "Just make it nice and neat." He said, "You know that means I will have to take it all off?" I looked at him through the mirror and said, "Do it." He turned my chair from facing the mirror and I closed my eyes as he started to cut. The buzzing noise was actually soothing. I could hear the voices of the people in the shop carrying on their conversations. I was waiting to hear whispers or for someone to ask what happened, but no one paid me any attention - except for Angie. I opened my eyes for a second and looked at her. Her eyes were watery. I closed my eyes; I could not be a part of that. As clear as I was about my decision, I was still nervous, and I was not quite sure what her tears meant.

After about 20 minutes, the buzzing stopped. He brushed the cut hair from my face and the apron he had placed around my body. He turned me back toward the mirror and said open your eyes. I slowly opened my eyes and looked in the mirror. I stared at myself for what seemed like forever. I turned my head back and forth, looking at my side profiles. I noticed Angie looking at me, still with water in her eyes. The barber broke the silence and said, "I like it. It looks hot on you." I smiled and said, "I like it too." Angie gave a sigh of relief and agreed.

As I got up out his chair and paid him, and was ready to leave, Angie asked if I wanted my scarf. I looked outside and said, "Nope. Let's go." When I stepped outside, the sun was shining and there was a gently breeze blowing. The mixture of sun and breeze hit my scalp for the first time in over 10 years, and it felt like what I believe feels like the windows of heaven opened and the angels began to sing. It was an amazing feeling; so freeing. I had been in bondage for so long and the feeling of freedom was almost overwhelming. It felt amazing!

Me and the Captain of Team Williams

For Men Only!

L adies, I know you saw the chapter said for men only, so if you are reading this, please feel free to excuse yourself and go to the next chapter.

I want to pause right here and talk to the men. I need you to help me out and let us get an understanding.. You love our hair as much as we do, and if the truth be told, you play a big part in this hair games as much as we do. How do I know? Because some of you always have a comment - whether for or against what we are doing with our hair. You have contributed to our hair games financial, emotionally, and spiritually. Our styles are often influenced by what you claim to like or prefer. You have contributed to what is acceptable and beautiful.

I can tell some of you are uncomfortable with these statements, but if you take a minute and get out of your feelings, I will explain. Now, before you shut down, let me say I am in no way blaming you, because we (women) must learn to stop allowing ALL outside influences to determine our beauty. I do not blame you, but I do want to talk about the influence you have and the part it plays in some of the confusion some women feel when it comes to their hair.

Now, I am directing this to the brothers. For years, we have all have been told the lie that something is wrong with the hair that grows naturally out of our scalp. We were told that it needed taming as if it was some type of wild creature. Society has constantly portrayed beautiful women as women with long hair and light skin. Social media has taken it to an entirely different level. Not only is beauty about long hair or light skin, but beauty is tiny, with big boobs and a big behind. Follow me because I am not bashing. These women are beautiful, but they are one type of beauty; there are many types.

When I first started going outside with my head shaved, you were the first to embrace me; men loved the look. You all were more accepting of it than some women. It was not trending when I cut my hair. It was different and you guys made sure to let me know you liked it. You guys stopped me in malls, markets, and on the street to let me know how nice I looked. You asked me who cut my hair and how I kept it so tight. You complimented me on the shape of my head and how fly I looked rocking my cut. Outside of my husband, you all helped me embrace the real me. I am not claiming that all of you loved my cut, but for the most part, the men were digging it. It is because of this I decided to talk to you.

Over the years that I have embraced my beauty mark (I no longer see my bald head as a flaw), I have met countless women who want to free themselves from wigs and weaves, but they claim their significant other is "not with it." Now, I already talked about how I struggled with telling my husband because I made up my mind that he would not agree. I did not believe he could be attracted to me or love me the same without my hair. When I finally sat down and actually talked to him about it, he was offended. He said he loved me, not my hair. I realize that my husband does not speak for all men, so I wanted to have a conversation.

When I asked these women if they talked to their husbands/significant other about wanting to free themselves, the majority of them say he doesn't like short hair, or he is not going to go for it. The women who come to me are not coming to me to talk about hair as a fashion statement. These are women who have either Alopecia or some other type of hair challenge. These women struggle with wanting to come from under these wigs and weaves, but because of what they think the man will say (or do), have said or implied, they chose to stay in bondage. My question is, how is it that you can support other women who walk out in their confidence, but you cannot support the women that support you? Why is it okay for someone else's woman but not for yours? Help us understand.

Hair type has been a mark of status for many years. Women with long hair have been favored over those with short or natural hair. Women (and some men) have been forced to wear their hair certain ways to be accepted in the marketplace and corporate America. We should not have to deal with the same bully at home and in our communities, especially from the males we constantly support. For black woman, the challenges we have endured because of our hair has been unbelievable. I remember watching Chris Rock's "Good Hair" documentary that looked at black women and our hair, and the billions of dollars we spend yearly to maintain our beautiful mains. I remember feeling sad watching it, as we saw little girls beginning the transformation process at a young age, simply to fit in. These babies are being taught at an early age that something is wrong with the hair that is naturally growing out of their head.

When my dad saw me for the first time without hair, he looked at me for a few seconds and then said, "Well, at least you are cute." In his mind, that was a compliment. What I heard was, "I don't like it." All my life, all I heard from my dad, in terms of my looks, was that I was so pretty. It did not have to be a special occasion. I did not have to be dressed up. My hair could actually be a mess, but he always made sure I knew he loved me and the way I looked. Imagine, years later, this same person, who helped build my confidence, looked at me and said, "Well, at least you are cute." He was not feeling it at all. This was his way of him reminding me I was cute. A back handed compliment that I would only accept from him. The difference here was, he had raised me to believe I was beautiful, and I believed it. By the time I took control of Alopecia, there was no doubt in my mind that I was beautiful.

I realized my husband may not be the norm. He loves me enough to be my biggest supporter. Unlike my father, he loved my cut, and his support only made me more confident, which in turn, I believe made me even more attractive to him. I am grateful to God that He had assigned Calvin as my husband, and he sees me – not just my hair. I am blessed that he is attracted to me with my bald head, but even more blessed that he was able support me through this process.

I do not take the fact that everyone has a preference. Granted we are all attracted to what we like. My husband is a butt man. I might be writing a different book if I lost my butt (just joking). I just want to challenge those who only see from one lens. Those of you who chose to go with the norm to look beyond the sociality expectations, consider how you would feel if your daughter doubted herself because of what she thought some knuckle head thought of her. Ok, I apologize. No name calling, but can we agree that these hair games are played out and rock with us as we wear our hair however the heck we please? I promise if you let her be who she is meant to be, you will reap the benefit.

Me and Big Daddy

Hair Does Not Define Me

The confidence and boldness that you all see in me are directly related to the women in my family. My entire life, I have been under the influence of some pretty dope women. These women are some of the strongest and baddest women to walk the planet, and I am blessed to call them family. These women have molded me and, with the help of God, have created what you see today. These women did their own thing demonstrating strength, power, determination, faith, and fearlessness. They laid a foundation that allowed me to boldly be who I was created to me.

These women are what we would call *gangster*. They were always on their game, and if they weren't, I never saw it. They spoke their minds and said what they said – PERIOD! When I was going through my season of depression, I remembered how I watched each of them walk through life challenges without missing a beat. They did not walk around beat down or looking for sympathy. They all walked out of their dark season with their heads up high with no resemblance of what they had been through. These are the women I look up to and gleam from. The ones whose blood run through my veins, whose sweet paved the way, and whose tears made them strong. All of the fierceness was deposited in me. I have no choice but to win!

Let me introduce you to my Dream Team. First up, hailing from the school of "Boss Chicks," is my great-grandmother who we lovingly called Ge-Ge. She lived life on her own terms. Traveling the world and then integrating a white neighbor, setting up roots for years to come. Imagine a black woman in the 50s moving into a white neighborhood with a maid to wash her clothes and clean her house (because she could). I always imagine what her attitude was, I wish a n__ would say something. Somewhat of neat freak, her house was always spotless. She could cook anything, and she was one of the best storytellers. She lived life with style and grace and could care less about what people thought about her. If she wanted to do something, she did it offering no explanation. She will forever be my original OG!

Next up is my dad's mom. Until I knew better (or someone finally corrected me), I called her Berta. Grandma-Bert moved next door to Ge-Ge, having the nerve to open a hair salon in the front of her house. This woman of God could chew you up and spit you out while praying down your healing all in the same breath. She was a strong black woman who called the shots. Inspiring generations to come. What inspired her to open her own business in an area and time that was not welcoming to people who looked like her? I believe it was because she wanted to, so she did it. I learned from her that you have to create the life you want to live.

Next up, the pint-sized ball of fire; my mother's mom who I call Mom-mom. She is always the leader of the pack. She was the first of nine children. She had a drive and work ethic that allowed her to have access to things that not many women, let alone black woman, were able to do. She married young and raised her three children while she climbed the corporate latter, until she became the HNIC. Growing up, I thought she was rich. She lived in a beautiful home, she vacationed, she had the best dinner parties for the holidays, and she always showered me with gift. She was the one who taught me the value of a dollar and the importance of paying my bills on time. Never one to waste a dollar when she would take me shopping; we'd go to high-end stores and she'd teach me the difference between fads, trends, and pieces that hold value. Not one to bite her tongue. You always know where she is coming from; she plays no games and I love it. She taught me to say what I mean and mean what I say.

Then there is my mom. My real day one. The master of minding your own business. The one who taught me the meaning of "If you like it, I love it." Always faithful and always ready! No one has had more influence on me than she has. She is tiny but mighty. She was a teenaged mother but has always been wise beyond her years. Always putting her family first, she has always been my biggest cheerleader and encourager. Always prepared with a gently word to calm me down, but always ready if need be. She is rarely, if ever, shaken. Don't let her small, calm demeanor fool you. She could yoke you up in three seconds flat. She does life on her own terms. Never moved by what people had to say. Always doing things her way (cause seriously, who gone check her). She is the glue that holds us all together. My dad always says you are just like your mother, and it's the best compliment he could give me. She's the real Rock Star!

These four helped me grow into the person you see today. It was because of their perceived strength that when I went through my depression, I went through it in silence. I kept thinking I needed to be like them. I needed to be strong. I needed to keep it together. This thinking only showed my immaturity. Of course, they probably had helped, and they had issues, but because they did not share them, I did not know it. All I constantly saw from them was "STRONG." And because of this, I kept telling myself that I needed to man up and be strong like them, and to deal with my stuff. So, I walked alone and got comfortable pretending and wearing my mask.

As blessed as I was to have this strong tribe of people around me, it made it hard for me to say I needed help. They had imparted so much into me and were so proud of me that I did not want to let them down. Hindsight is 20-20, and I know this was just my fears again creating false scenarios to keep me in bondage. The last thing this group of women would have done was judge me. In fact, they would have rallied around me to help me become whole.

It was because of this I decided to be open with my daughters. Having all the strong characteristics of the women that came before me and I never wanted my daughters to feel like they needed to pretend to be ok if they were not. If they were ever going through something or were struggling with something, I wanted them to know it was okay, and that I am always here. I practiced talking to them about everything. Not just my achievements, but also my mistakes and my failures. I chose to be an open book with them so that they would know that although I was strong, I was vulnerable, and I too have my weaknesses. This openness helped us to develop a friendship as they became young adults.

It was actually because of my oldest I started sharing my story on a larger scale. In her junior year of college, she had the opportunity to teach art in a local school. One of her 4th grade students came to school every day with a wig. My daughter described her as one of the sweetest little girls, but that she was wearing a wig. Because store-brought wigs are not made for kids, it was obvious she had one on, and some of the kids teased her. She was told that some even attempted to snatch it off.

By the time my daughter was teaching art, I was comfortable with my baldness. She told me about her student and asked if I would come and talk to her. We scheduled a surprise lunch date. The day of lunch, I arrived early and was waiting in the lunchroom for my date. When the kids entered the lunchroom, the kids started looking around and asking each other, "Who is that?" I finally saw the young lady walk in. I walked over to her and introduced myself. Her eyes opened as if she was in shock, and a huge smile came across her face. I invited her to sit down, and we began to talk.

She was full of questions about my hair and how I did become comfortable enough to come outside without covering my head. We talked so much that she forgot to eat. While we were talking, her friends kept staring and smiling at us. Some called out to her, asking who I was. I finally asked her if she wanted some of her friends to join us, and she agreed and called them over. Ten little girls rushed our table, all giggles, and smiles. They began to ask a million questions about what happened to my hair.

We turned this lunch hour into a teachable moment. Not only were the girls at the lunch table listening to our conversation, but all the kids in the lunchroom were curious as to who this bald woman was. I shared with them what Alopecia Areata was an autoimmune disease that causes a person's hair to fall out, and that there was no cure. Then I opened up the floor to questions. Those kids shot off those questions like ammunition in an AK 47. The questions were non-stop, and I loved it. Next thing you knew, lunch was over, and the kids did not want to leave. I was asked if I would come back again to share with the students, and of course I said yes.

The next day, I received a call from the principal of my daughter's school. I was a little nervous to talk to her because I didn't know what to expect. Of course, my wild imagination started creating all kinds of negative scenarios. Nonetheless, I answered the call and the principal began to tell me that "our friend" came to school today without her wig and announced to everyone that, "This was her. Take it or leave it." She had gained a confidence that they had not seen, and they thanked me for coming to share my story. I can't tell how this made me feel, but I felt so proud. She had no idea what it took for me to get there, but it didn't matter; I had finally tapped into who I was meant to be.

I remember one evening, after speaking at an event, a woman can up to me and said, "Thank you for sharing your story. You really got me." I stared at her for a while and thought to myself, "what did I say that would make you believe I got you??" I was confused because the tall, black woman standing before was missing a nose. She stood in front of me, with two holes in the middle of her face where her nose should have been, smiling and telling me I got her. "How sway," I remember thinking. She said, "Thank you for reminding us that we all have our own challenges and we all have our own journey. Thank you for saying we need to love ourselves – flaws and all." I then told the audience that I had learned to love myself so much that I no longer saw my bald head as a flaw, but I learn to accept it as my beauty mark. The beauty mark of our culture is actually a mark of magnificence that is often overlooked. This woman actually helped me to see this thing clearly. My story was not really about hair, but it was more about one learning to love themselves just the way they are. Self-acceptance is one of the most beautiful things you can have.

It's crazy how there is nothing really new under the sun. When Africans were stolen and brought here, the first thing the colonizers did was strip us of our identity. They separated us and stole our language, changed our names, and made us feel like we were less than human. As our ancestors stood in all their glory, they were told that they were animals. The lie was told so much that many believed it and passed it on to their children. We brought the lie that our color, our body shapes, and our hair was foul. They brainwashed us, and to this day, we still struggle with accepting ourselves.

I am not saying this self-acceptance journey is easy, because it's not. It is so much easier to go along with the crowd and not stand out. It is why some people just go with the flow and never come to full realization of who they really are. It's sad because we never get to see the real you, until you are willing to do the work to become who you were meant to be.

Who would have thought by losing my hair, one thing I always wanted, would push me into my destiny? Although I was caught off guard by my loss of hair, God was not. He wasn't the least bit surprised. He knew that I would one day be bald, and that I would share my story to help women show what's is possible in spite of, and to own what makes them unique and different. Own who you are! There is no one like you, and no one can do you better than you. It is a gift waiting to be opened and shared with the world. Someone is waiting for you.

Welcome to my life, it's so me. Now go and be you!

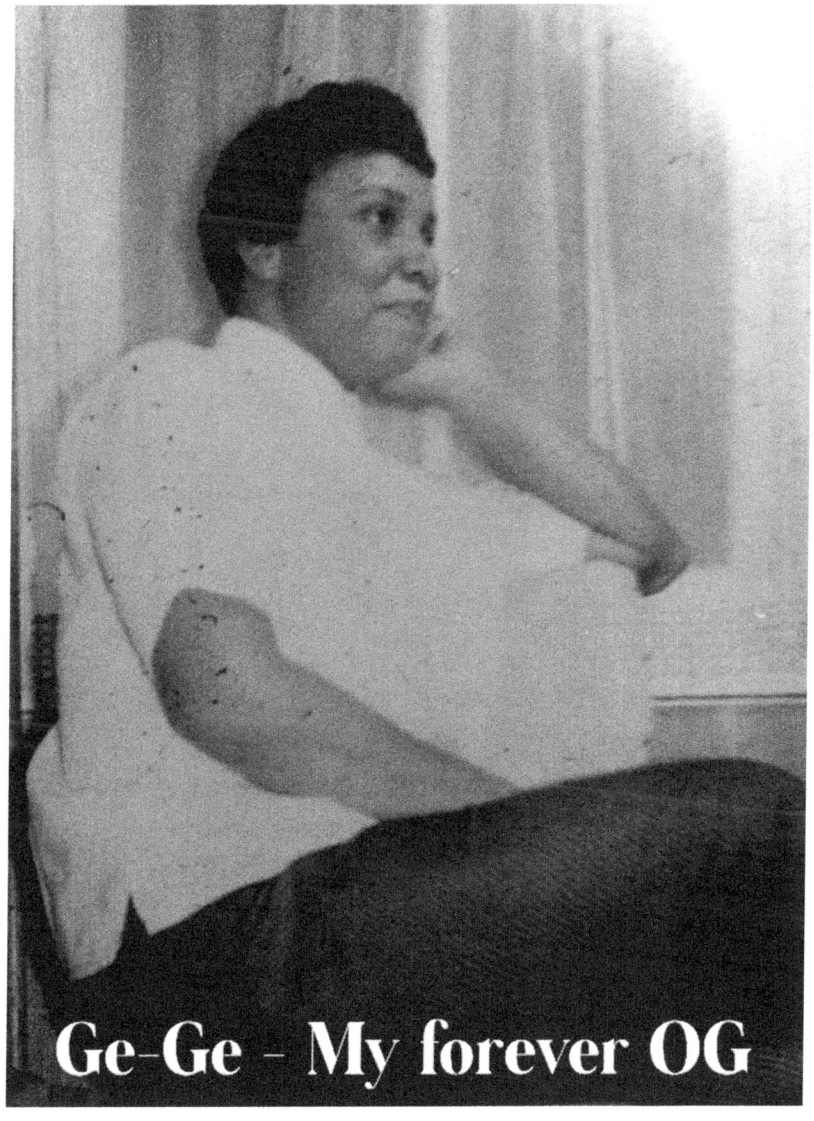

Ge-Ge - My forever OG

The Master Presser

Me and My favorite Girl

Mom-Mom and Mommy

Mom-Mom - The Boss

Epilogue

I never want to minimize others' feelings because I know that people genuinely struggle with hair loss. Although I feel free without hair, that is not everyone's testimony. As you just read, it was a long journey for me to get here. The choice to cut one's hair is a very personal decision that is usually not entered into lightly – especially if it is not by choice. People need to make the best decision for themselves without outside influence from others who have no nickel in their dime. I did not write this book to shame or guilt anyone into cutting their hair or wearing a wig. The purpose of me writing the book is just the opposite. I want people to own who they are and be comfortable in it. If that means rocking a wig or weave, do it. If that means embracing your bald head, then rock on with your bald self.

Beauty is not defined by one style or type. Beauty is wrapped in the uniqueness of who you are. How boring would life be if we all looked the same? How closed-minded are we to believe that only thin, lighter-skinned, and long-haired women should be the standard of beauty? It is time for that lie to die. When our ancestors were stolen and brought here, the male colonizers publicly denounced us, while privately craving our chocolate skin, wide hips, and tightly curled hair. Our ancestors endured more than we could ever imagine. I honor them with my natural hair or lack thereof. No one will ever define what beauty is for me. Hair is not a necessity – it is only an accessory. The world we live in is full of so many beautiful types of people created in the image of a loving Father, and we all need to be celebrated. To those who are yet to see their beauty, I'm here for you, and I see you, and yes, you are also beautiful.

CONGRATULATIONS

To My First 50 Pre-Order Supporters

Beatrice Johnson

Nikki Estrada

Kena Cooper

Calische Gully

AuRelia Mauldin

TyRae Freeman

Blaine Jones

Helen Jones

Portia Taylor

Chenelle Pettiford

Theresa Royal Brown

Shakara Dalecki

Lena Wilson

Dominick Thurston

Tasha Butler

Niah Minott

Margaret Slobasky

Marsha Frazier

Santosha Troutman

Constance Miles

Audrey McLaurin

Kamela Smith

Anika Dixon

Eleanor Doris

Lisa A. Chin

Patricia Williams, Mother in Law

Martha Spencer

Dana Harris

Michael Daniels aka MIKEYBLAZE

Shun Strickland

Tracy Stewart

Teressa Bonner

Theresa Butler

Erika Ragland-Lee

Aunt Donna Odums

Aunt Donna Odums

Khadiyjah Anderson

Damali Thomas

Cynthia M. Hayward

Brandi Crawford

Courtney Haywood, M. Ed.

Lisa Carter

Janay Harris

Bettina Moore

Kim Perry

Dawn A Roberts

Shaniqua Hill

Erica J. Murray

Tyrice McCoy

Ti Kendrick Randall

Anglean Walton

About Bald Girl Inc.

Bald Girl Inc. is an organization designed to redefine society's view of beauty, and to help women recognize their true beauty by assisting them in realizing that they are more than their hair. Bald Girl was birthed after Lorraine Williams overcame her fear of Alopecia Areata and wanted to create a safe place for bald women, or women who were losing their hair to heal.

Conversations with Bald Girl
PODCAST HOSTED BY LORRAINE WILLIAMS

Instagram: @conversationswithbaldgirl
Facebook: Bald Girl Inc

Made in the USA
Monee, IL
31 October 2020

46401856R00066